Who Am I?
Leeds United Quiz Book
Guess The Career Path

FIRSTPRINTFOOTBALL.COM

Introduction

First Print Football's *Guess The Career Path* consists of 100 "Who am I?" questions. Every page details a former player's football club history from beginning to end. Your job is simple: guess the footballer.

Guess The Career Path is one of the most popular quiz games among football fans. Even if you're unsure of an answer, you can at least take an educated guess simply based on a player's past clubs and career span.

Answers can be found at the back of the book.

Good luck!

Danny Hart | First Print Football

Disclaimer

This book is unofficial and does not claim to be affiliated with any football clubs or people mentioned in the questions and answers.

PLAYER 1

Leeds United
Levante
Sunderland
Blackpool
Carlisle United
Reading
AFC Bournemouth

Career: 1996-2015

PLAYER 2

Mallorca B
Ciudad de Murcia (loan)
Terrassa
Barcelona B
Merida
Leeds United
Norwich City
Rotherham United (loan)
Club Atletico Belgrano
Rotherham United
Atletico Baleares
Binissalem

Career: 2003-2017

PLAYER 3

Leeds United
Everton
Newcastle United
Bolton Wanderers
Sheffield United

Career: 1988-2010

PLAYER 4

Leeds United
Hull City
Doncaster Rovers

Career: 1960-1982

PLAYER 5

Manchester United
Port Vale (loan)
Preston North End (loan)
Preston North End
Norwich City (loan)
Norwich City (loan)
Leeds United
Fulham
Sunderland
Ipswich Town (loan)
Doncaster Rovers (loan)
Rangers
Bury

Career: 1999-2013

PLAYER 6

Wealdstone
IFK Holmsund (loan)
Wimbledon
Leeds United
Sheffield United
Chelsea
Wimbledon
Queens Park Rangers

Career: 1984-1999

PLAYER 7

Leeds United
Bristol City
Barnsley

Career: 1962-1982

PLAYER 8

Auxerre
Martigues (loan)
Marseille
Bordeaux (loan)
Montpellier (loan)
Nimes
Leeds United (loan)
Leeds United
Manchester United

Career: 1983-1997

PLAYER 9

Sochaux
Rennes
Lens
Liverpool
Bolton Wanderers (loan)
Bolton Wanderers
Sunderland
Blackburn Rovers
Rangers (loan)
Doncaster Rovers
Leeds United
Sabah FA

Career: 1998-2015

PLAYER 10

Telstar
AZ Alkmaar
Neerlandia
Campomaiorense
Boavista
Leeds United
Atletico Madrid
Chelsea
Middlesbrough
Charlton Athletic
Cardiff City

Career: 1990-2008

PLAYER 11

Bryne FK
Nottingham Forest
Leeds United
Manchester City
Bryne FK
Rosseland BK

Career: 1989-2003, 2011-2013

PLAYER 12

Tottenham Hotspur
Middlesbrough
Everton
Liverpool
Leeds United
Nottingham Forest (loan)
Hull City

Career: 1992-2012

PLAYER 13

Leeds United
Manchester United
Newcastle United
Milton Keynes Dons (loan)
Milton Keynes Dons
Notts County

Career: 1998-2018

PLAYER 14

Leeds United
Coventry City
Tottenham Hotspur
Vancouver Whitecaps
Bradford City
Swansea City

Career: 1967-1986

PLAYER 15

Dundee
Aberdeen
Manchester United
Leeds United
Coventry City

Career: 1974-1997

PLAYER 16

York City
Mansfield Town (loan)
Sheffield Wednesday
Leicester City
Preston North End (loan)
Preston North End
Leeds United
Stoke City
Sheffield United (loan)
Sheffield United
York City (loan)
York City
Tadcaster Albion

Career: 1995-2017

PLAYER 17

Strasbourg
Everton
Lens
Leeds United
Roma (loan)
Roma
Inter Milan
Fulham (loan)
Standard Liege

Career: 1992-2010

PLAYER 18

Leeds United
Tottenham Hotspur
Everton (loan)
Everton
Burnley
Kayserispor
Burnley

Career: 2003-2022

PLAYER 19

Sunderland
Leeds United
Newcastle United (loan)
Bolton Wanderers
Sunderland (loan)
Sunderland
Bristol City
Carlisle United (loan)
Carlisle United
Hull City
Sydney FC (loan)
Carlisle United (loan)
Milton Keynes Dons
Newcastle Jets
Lambton Jaffas

Career: 1995-2015

PLAYER 20

Liverpool
Sunderland (loan)
Leeds United
Blackburn Rovers
Stoke City

Career: 1992-2009

PLAYER 21

Notts County
Sheffield United
Portsmouth
Crystal Palace
Nottingham Forest (loan)
Leeds United
Crystal Palace (loan)
Crystal Palace
Queens Park Rangers
Millwall (loan)
Notts County

Career: 1995-2015

PLAYER 22

Leeds United
West Ham United (loan)
Sheffield United
Sunderland
Middlesbrough (loan)
Doncaster Rovers (loan)
Blackburn Rovers
Bradford City
Hamilton Academical
Hyderabad
Buxton

Career: 2002-2021

PLAYER 23

Leeds United
Nottingham Forest
Leeds United
Sunderland
Darlington

Career: 1972-1992

PLAYER 24

Chelsea
Bournemouth (loan)
Leeds United
Stoke City (loan)
Stoke City
Reading
Wycombe Wanderers
St Johnstone
Oxford United
Hendon

Career: 1993-2013

PLAYER 25

Vitoria Setubal
Leeds United
Sheffield United
Uniao de Leiria (loan)
Beira-Mar
Santa Clara
Vitoria Setubal
Chaves (loan)

Career: 1994-2010

PLAYER 26

Leeds United
Bradford City
Newcastle KB United

Career: 1962-1981

PLAYER 27

Leeds United
Juventus
Leeds United
Roma
Cardiff City
Hereford United
Merthyr Tydfil

Career: 1949-1974

PLAYER 28

Manchester City
Hartlepool United (loan)
Portsmouth (loan)
Sheffield United (loan)
Sheffield United
Tottenham Hotspur
Fulham
Wigan Athletic
Portsmouth
Leeds United
Port Vale

Career: 1994-2017

PLAYER 29

Leeds United
Newcastle United
Real Madrid
Middlesbrough (loan)
Middlesbrough
Tottenham Hotspur
Stoke City
Middlesbrough

Career: 1998-2016

PLAYER 30

Leeds United
Arsenal
Leeds United
Arsenal

Career: 1978-2001

PLAYER 31

Leeds United
Oldham Athletic
Manchester United
Wolverhampton Wanderers

Career: 1983-2004

PLAYER 32

Leeds United
Stoke City (loan)
Stoke City (loan)
Charlton Athletic
Southampton
Middlesbrough
Ipswich Town (loan)
Rotherham United
Doncaster Rovers

Career: 2001-2016

PLAYER 33

Leeds United

Career: 1992-2007

PLAYER 34

Koge BK
Brondby IF
Leeds United (loan)
Leeds United
Brighton & Hove Albion

Career: 1998-2017

PLAYER 35

Wolverhampton Wanderers
Coventry City
Inter Milan
Leeds United (loan)
Leeds United
Tottenham Hotspur
Liverpool
Tottenham Hotspur
Celtic (loan)
West Ham United (loan)
LA Galaxy
Aston Villa (loan)
ATK

Career: 1997-2018

PLAYER 36

West Ham United
AFC Bournemouth (loan)
Leeds United
Manchester United
Queens Park Rangers

Career: 1995-2015

PLAYER 37

Wimbledon
Crystal Palace (loan)
Tottenham Hotspur
Chelsea
Leeds United
Doncaster Rovers (loan)
Doncaster Rovers (loan)
Doncaster Rovers
AFC Wimbledon (loan)

Career: 1988-2013

PLAYER 38

FC Baden
SSV Ulm
Hertha BSC
VfB Stuttgart (loan)
VfB Stuttgart
Maritimo
Leeds United
Hull City (loan)

Career: 1998-2010

PLAYER 39

Leeds United
Tottenham Hotspur
Blackburn Rovers
Burnley

Career: 1998-2017

PLAYER 40

Leeds United
Blackburn Rovers
Newcastle United
Leeds United

Career: 1987-2004

PLAYER 41

Leeds United
Aston Villa
Leeds United (loan)
Manchester City
Everton

Career: 2006-2022

PLAYER 42

Ballymena United
Notts County
Sheffield Wednesday
Leeds United
Stoke City
Blackpool

Career: 1979-1998

PLAYER 43

Asante Kotoko
Cornerstones Kumasi
Okwawu United
1. FC Saarbrucken
Eintracht Frankfurt
Leeds United
Hamburger SV
Al-Ittihad

Career: 1981-2002

PLAYER 44

San Jose Clash
Fulham
Preston North End
Leeds United
Derby County
Los Angeles Galaxy

Career: 1996-2010

PLAYER 45

Leeds United
Liverpool
Galatasaray
Melbourne Victory
Al-Gharafa
Melbourne Heart

Career: 1996-2014

PLAYER 46

Blackpool
Queens Park Rangers
Leeds United
Watford
Luton Town (loan)
Burnley
Preston North End (loan)
Northampton Town (loan)
York City
Northampton Town (loan)
Northampton Town

Career: 1997-2013

PLAYER 47

Melbourne Knights
Dinamo Zagreb
Celtic
Leeds United
Middlesbrough
Newcastle United

Career: 1993-2009

PLAYER 48

Arsenal
Crystal Palace (loan)
New York Express
Los Angeles Lazers
West Bromwich Albion
Leeds United
Birmingham City
Coventry City (loan)
West Ham United (loan)
Charlton Athletic
Detroit Neon
Detroit Safari
Leyton Orient
Oxford United
Rushden & Diamonds
Raleigh Express
Harlow Town
HyPS

Career: 1978-2000

PLAYER 49

Bradford Park Avenue
Bury
Whitby Town (loan)
Sheffield United (loan)
Sheffield United
Queens Park Rangers
Leeds United
Bolton Wanderers
Oldham Athletic (loan)
Ipswich Town
Bury
Rotherham United
Northampton Town
Maltby Main

Career: 1997-2018

PLAYER 50

Celtic
Southampton
Leeds United
Blackpool
Wigan Athletic
Fleetwood Town
AFC Fylde

Career: 1997-2016

PLAYER 51

Rochdale
Bury
Sunderland
Wolverhampton Wanderers (loan)
Wolverhampton Wanderers
Leeds United
Milton Keynes Dons (loan)
Milton Keynes Dons
Chester City

Career: 1991-2009

PLAYER 52

Morton
Leeds United
Manchester United
AC Milan
Hellas Verona
Southampton
Bristol City

Career: 1968-1989

PLAYER 53

Nasvikens IK
GIF Sundsvall
IFK Norrkoping
Parma
Leeds United
FC Zurich (loan)
Parma (loan)
Crystal Palace
Hudiksvalls ABK

Career: 1984-1998

PLAYER 54

Spalding United
Sheffield Wednesday
Bristol City
Leeds United
Malmo FF (loan)
Birmingham City
Manchester City (loan)
Bradford City
Darlington
Kettering Town
Bradford Park Avenue

Career: 1982-2005

PLAYER 55

Nottingham Forest
Tottenham Hotspur
Leeds United (loan)
Leeds United
Bolton Wanderers
Notts County
York City (loan)
York City

Career: 1981-2001

PLAYER 56

Arsenal
Leeds United
Manchester City
Chelsea
Norwich City (loan)
Hull City (loan)
Sabah

Career: 1985-1999

PLAYER 57

Bristol Rovers
Crystal Palace
Leeds United
Everton

Career: 1987-2006

PLAYER 58

Blackburn Rovers
Oldham Athletic (loan)
Birmingham City
Oldham Athletic (loan)
Sheffield Wednesday (loan)
Tranmere Rovers (loan)
Ipswich Town
Leicester City (loan)
Leeds United
Huddersfield Town (loan)
Hull City
Wigan Athletic (loan)
Bury
Wigan Athletic
Kilmarnock
Macclesfield

Career: 2004-2022

PLAYER 59

Leeds United
Cape Town City (loan)
Toronto Blizzard
York City
Toronto Blizzard
Vancouver Whitecaps
UCD (loan)
Leeds United
Whitby Town
Hapoel Haifa

Career: 1962-1986

PLAYER 60

Norwich City
Charlton Athletic
Leeds United
Middlesbrough (loan)
Manchester City
Hull City (loan)
Charlton Athletic (loan)
Derby County (loan)

Career: 1994-2009

PLAYER 61

Brescia
Sampdoria
Leeds United
Sion
Bellinzona

Career: 2007-2023

PLAYER 62

Kaizer Chiefs
Leeds United

Career: 1989-2005

PLAYER 63

Manchester City
Leeds United
Nottingham Forest
Sheffield Wednesday
Birmingham City (loan)
Bolton Wanderers (loan)
Bolton Wanderers
Doncaster Rovers
Oldham Athletic

Career: 1981-2004

PLAYER 64

Aston Villa
Chelsea
Leeds United
Torino
Derby County
Stoke City

Career: 1984-2001

PLAYER 65

Oldham Athletic
Notts County
Reading
Norwich City
Leeds United
Scunthorpe United
Charlton Athletic
Bolton Wanderers

Career: 1996-2015

PLAYER 66

Manchester United
Leeds United
West Bromwich Albion
Philadelphia Fury
Shamrock Rovers

Career: 1957-1983

PLAYER 67

Crewe Alexandra
Hyde United (loan)
West Bromwich Albion
Leeds United (loan)
Leeds United
Sheffield United
Derby County
Queens Park Rangers
Charlton Athletic (loan)

Career: 1998-2013

PLAYER 68

FC Volendam
Leeds United
Bradford City
RBC Roosendaal

Career: 1992-2007

PLAYER 69

Crewe Alexandra
Derby County
Leeds United
Derby County

Career: 1996-2007

PLAYER 70

West Ham United
Orient
Aston Villa
Leeds United
Luton Town (loan)
Sheffield United (loan)
Carlisle United

Career: 1973-1994

PLAYER 71

Sheffield Wednesday
Leeds United
Bradford City

Career: 1989-2008

PLAYER 72

Sogndal
Tromso
Brann
Chelsea
Rangers
Sunderland
Siena
Valerenga
Leeds United
Milton Keynes Dons
Sogndal

Career: 1993-2012

PLAYER 73

Leeds United
Vancouver Whitecaps
Leeds United
Drogheda United (loan)
Vancouver Whitecaps
Leeds United
Partick Thistle
Bradford City
Whitby Town
Morton
Harrogate Town

Career: 1965-1987

PLAYER 74

Paris Saint-Germain
Dunfermline Athletic
Hibernian
Leicester City
Trabzonspor
Palermo
Leeds United (loan)
Leeds United
Cardiff City
Middlesbrough

Career: 2004-2022

PLAYER 75

Greenock Morton
Chelsea
Crystal Palace
Leeds United
Bradford City
Crystal Palace
Greenock Morton

Career: 1989-2003

PLAYER 76

Manchester United
Leeds United
Preston North End
Stoke City (loan)
Stoke City
Preston North End (loan)
Leeds United (loan)
Leeds United
Sheffield Wednesday (loan)
Coventry City
Bury
Blackpool
Port Vale
Hanley Town

Career: 2000-2022

PLAYER 77

Liverpool
Leeds United
Manchester City
Liverpool
Cardiff City
Blackburn Rovers
North Queensland Fury
Perth Glory
Muangthong United

Career: 1993-2012

PLAYER 78

Lincoln City
Newcastle United
Millwall (loan)
Coventry City
Leeds United
Manchester City
Nottingham Forest (loan)
Norwich City (loan)
Norwich City
San Jose Earthquakes

Career: 1993-2009

PLAYER 79

Sheffield Wednesday
Rangers
Leeds United
Boston United

Career: 1978-1996

PLAYER 80

Portsmouth
Swindon Town
Portsmouth
Brentford
Swindon Town
Stoke City
Leeds United
Luton Town
Sheffield United (loan)
Middlesbrough (loan)
Sheffield United
Bradford City

Career: 1975-1995

PLAYER 81

Blackburn Rovers
Leeds United
Leicester City
Blackpool (loan)
Blackpool

Career: 1989-2006

PLAYER 82

Doncaster Rovers
Sheffield United
Leeds United
Sheffield United
Benfica
Middlesbrough
Leicester City
West Ham United
Leeds United
Sunderland
Perth Glory
Sheffield United

Career: 1985-2006

PLAYER 83

Nottingham Forest
Southampton
Nottingham Forest (loan)
Leeds United
Colchester United (loan)
Colchester United
Swindon Town
Sheffield Wednesday
Scunthorpe United (loan)
Coventry City (loan)

Career: 1998-2014

PLAYER 84

Doncaster Rovers
Sheffield Wednesday
Leeds United
Oldham Athletic (loan)
Rotherham United (loan)
Hearts
Barnsley
Gainsborough Trinity

Career: 1977-1998

PLAYER 85

Darlington
Waterford United (loan)
Bradford City
Nottingham Forest (loan)
Burnley
Birmingham City
Leeds United
Burnley
Bolton Wanderers
Doncaster Rovers
Team Northumbria

Career: 1994-2013

PLAYER 86

Motherwell
Leicester City
Leeds United
Coventry City
Liverpool
Coventry City

Career: 1981-2004

PLAYER 87

Southampton
Leeds United
Rangers
Bolton Wanderers
Gillingham

Career: 1987-2004

PLAYER 88

Sheffield United
Leeds United

Career: 1963-1975

PLAYER 89

Charlton Athletic
Leeds United
West Ham United
Newcastle United
West Ham United
Birmingham City (loan)
Birmingham City
Ipswich Town

Career: 1994-2012

PLAYER 90

Valencia B
Onda (loan)
Valencia
Cadiz (loan)
Getafe
Valencia
Swansea City
Al-Arabi
Al-Nasr (loan)
Rayo Vallecano (loan)
Leeds United (loan)
Leeds United
Castellon

Career: 2004-2023

PLAYER 91

Jomo Cosmos
Mamelodi Sundowns
Leeds United
St. Gallen
Salernitana
Bari
Al-Wahda

Career: 1990-2002

PLAYER 92

St Mirren
Leeds United
Manchester United
Seiko

Career: 1970-1986

PLAYER 93

Stoke City
Plymouth Argyle (loan)
Arsenal
Sunderland
Sheffield Wednesday
Chamois Niortais
Nottingham Forest
Leeds United
Portsmouth
West Ham United
Southend United (loan)
Ipswich Town
Leeds United (loan)
Swansea City
Stromsgodset Toppfotball

Career: 1978-1996

PLAYER 94

Wealdstone
Uxbridge (loan)
Leeds United
Carlisle United (loan)
Scunthorpe United (loan)
Everton
Leicester City
Huddersfield Town (loan)
Bolton Wanderers
Preston North End (loan)
Preston North End
Bury

Career: 2003-2019

PLAYER 95

Leeds United

Career: 1952-1973

PLAYER 96

Blackburn Rovers
Chesterfield (loan)
Blackpool (loan)
Gillingham (loan)
Leeds United (loan)
Leeds United
Swindon Town
Brentford
Ipswich Town

Career: 2000-2017

PLAYER 97

Sogndal
Leeds United
Aston Villa (loan)
Brann
Sogndal

Career: 1993-2012

PLAYER 98

Huddersfield Town
Leeds United
Bradford City

Career: 1965-1985

PLAYER 99

Leeds United
Millwall (loan)
Nottingham Forest (loan)
Barnsley
Cardiff City
Sheffield Wednesday
Shamrock Rovers

Career: 1997-2016

PLAYER 100

Walsall
Fulham
Leicester City
Leeds United
Barnsley

Career: 1963-1980

ANSWERS 1-10

1. Ian Harte
2. Luciano Becchio
3. Gary Speed
4. Billy Bremner
5. David Healy
6. Vinnie Jones
7. Norman Hunter
8. Eric Cantona
9. El Hadji Diouf
10. Jimmy Floyd Hasselbaink

ANSWERS 11-20

11. Alfie Haaland
12. Nick Barmby
13. Alan Smith
14. Terry Yorath
15. Gordon Strachan
16. Richard Cresswell
17. Olivier Dacourt
18. Aaron Lennon
19. Michael Bridges
20. Dominic Matteo

ANSWERS 21-30

21. Shaun Derry
22. Matthew Kilgallon
23. Frank Gray
24. Michael Duberry
25. Bruno Ribeiro
26. Paul Reaney
27. John Charles
28. Michael Brown
29. Jonathan Woodgate
30. John Lukic

ANSWERS 31-40

31. Denis Irwin
32. Frazer Richardson
33. Gary Kelly
34. Casper Ankergren
35. Robbie Keane
36. Rio Ferdinand
37. Neil Sullivan
38. Rui Marques
39. Paul Robinson
40. David Batty

ANSWERS 41-50

41. Fabian Delph
42. Nigel Worthington
43. Tony Yeboah
44. Eddie Lewis
45. Harry Kewell
46. Clarke Carlisle
47. Mark Viduka
48. Chris Whyte
49. Paddy Kenny
50. Stephen Crainey

ANSWERS 51-60

51. Paul Butler
52. Joe Jordan
53. Tomas Brolin
54. Carl Shutt
55. Chris Fairclough
56. David Rocastle
57. Nigel Martyn
58. Alex Bruce
59. Peter Lorimer
60. Danny Mills

ANSWERS 61-70

61. Gaetano Berardi
62. Lucas Radebe
63. John Sheridan
64. Tony Dorigo
65. Andrew Hughes
66. Johnny Giles
67. Robert Hulse
68. Robert Molenaar
69. Seth Johnson
70. Mervyn Day

ANSWERS 71-80

71. David Wetherall
72. Tore Andre Flo
73. David Harvey
74. Sol Bamba
75. David Hopkin
76. Danny Pugh
77. Robbie Fowler
78. Darren Huckerby
79. Mel Sterland
80. Chris Kamara

ANSWERS 81-90

81. Jason Wilcox
82. Brian Deane
83. David Prutton
84. Glynn Snodin
85. Robbie Blake
86. Gary McAllister
87. Rod Wallace
88. Mick Jones
89. Lee Bowyer
90. Pablo Hernandez

ANSWERS 91-100

91. Phil Masinga
92. Gordon McQueen
93. Lee Chapman
94. Jermaine Beckford
95. Jack Charlton
96. Jonathan Douglas
97. Eirik Bakke
98. Trevor Cherry
99. Stephen McPhail
100. Allan Clarke

500 English Football
Quiz Questions
Available Now!

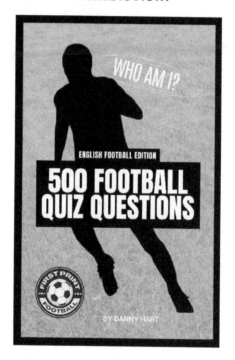

FIRSTPRINTFOOTBALL.COM